HE SAVED MY LIFE

HE SAVED MY LIFE

HOPE IN RECOVERY

Veronica Stoneall

authorHOUSE®

AuthorHouse™
1663 Liberty Drive
Bloomington, IN 47403
www.authorhouse.com
Phone: 1-800-839-8640

First published by AuthorHouse   10/13/2011

ISBN: 978-1-4670-4339-7 (sc)
ISBN: 978-1-4670-4343-4 (ebk)

Library of Congress Control Number: 2011917559

Printed in the United States of America

DEDICATED TO THOSE WHO

HAVE FOUND HOPE IN SOBRIETY

AND THOSE WHO SEEK IT

———————————————————————

IN MEMORY OF JIM STONEALL

To those who cared.

Introduction:

Jim was a man whose passion was helping others. His greatest joy was helping those afflicted with the disease of alcoholism or drug addiction. He understood the disease. He had lived through the hope, the destruction and the recovery of the disease. He was not able to conquer all the parts of his life, but could see into the hearts and souls of others and help them see what was necessary to live a sober life. Jim struggled daily with the power of alcohol and addiction. He made a decision to not drink every day and through the power of his higher power, Jesus Christ the God of the Universe, remained sober for nearly 30 years.

He was not always happy with his gifts, but came to know the power of his insights. He was always drawn to the person who was in trouble or in need of a helping hand. He was—just Jim—what you see is what you get. His sudden death caused an outpouring of love from those around him. Shock, disbelief and deep sadness came from those who knew him best. Jim had touched many people and through the guidance of his Lord and Savior had helped them find sobriety and a love of themselves. He genuinely cared.

Many times the words, "He saved my life" were spoken as people came with tears in their eyes to pay their respects to Jim.

These words of wisdom were found written in his handwriting on a piece of paper in his big book.

1. I am alcoholic. Nothing happens in God's world by mistake.
2. Examining the actions and motives of others is a waste of time.
3. The troubles of today are sufficient for today.
4. God has no intentions of an unreasonable nature of others and me—Follow God's lead.
5. Commit my life to God daily.
6. Make conscious contact with God often each day.
7. Remember God is in charge.
8. Be honest with me about who I really am and the dangers involved without a walk with God.
9. Keep God in the center of my world—everyone benefits.
10. Watch for negative, degrading self-talk—it gets projected on to others
11. Do not depend on laurels of past days. Each day stands on its own.

This is not a book about the way it was or the way it
should be, but the way he wanted it to be.

Jim's greatest desire was to have a life like what
he hoped each person who came into his life could
achieve.

He believed God could do this for each of us
if we let Him.

THE BEGINNING
AND THE END

SOBRIETY

HE SAVED MY LIFE:

With tears in their eyes they came and said, over and over, "He saved my life. It was because of him that I am sober today. He was a good man. I loved him. I am grateful to him."

> Sobriety: Grateful for one day at a time.
> Grateful for one moment at a time.
> Grateful for one second at a time.

Let go and Let God!

SELF-ESTEEM

HE SAVED MY LIFE:

He taught me I was worth staying sober. "I love ya, kid. Did I tell you that today?" Yes you did! Thank you!

Self-esteem: What is that? I didn't have any.
My higher power says I am a worthy person.
How do I believe it?
I have been so bad. I have done bad things.
I must forgive myself.

"God loves you. You must learn to love yourself."

SUFFERING

HE SAVED MY LIFE:

Hands on the shoulder, a big hug, steel blue eyes looking at me in the face saying, "You're ok. You can do it. Did I tell you today, I love you?"

> Suffering: Those who suffer from the disease
> of alcoholism often feel less than loved.
> Self-hatred—I am not worthy. I'm bad.
> No one can love me.

One man convinced many of his love for them. His passion was helping others find sobriety and learning to love themselves.

FRIENDSHIP

HE SAVED MY LIFE:

He was my sunshine. He treated me with respect.
I loved him dearly. He was my friend.

Friendship: A genuine caring for each other even
when the person is not always the
most loveable.

Friendship can be a new experience
after facing the depth of loneliness.

A big hug, a smile and a pat on the shoulder.

You are my friend.

SUCCESS

HE SAVED MY LIFE:

He was the first person I saw when I came to seek help. He welcomed me with open arms. (Literally, he was free with his hugs for almost everyone)

> Success: "Come in! Remember we do not condemn you. We want you to succeed. If I can make it, so can you. I will tell you my story."

"I am an alcoholic. I commit my day to God everyday. I ask God to help me stay sober today. With the help of my higher power (I choose to call Him God), I can do this. My life can become better. My life can become meaningful and my life can become my own. Yours can, too."

ADMISSION

HE SAVED MY LIFE:

It was a hot summer day. The humidity was 95%. The temperature was at least 97 degrees. The air conditioner was on. It was quite pleasant inside. Our wives were sitting in the cool living room.

"Let's grab a cup of coffee."

> Sure.
>
> We go out in the hot sun on the sun-drenched patio. It is 97 degrees! I have a hot cup of coffee!
>
> Whew! It is warm out here!

Admission: "Well, what do you think? Do you admit you have a drinking problem?"

> Well, ah, do you think so? Maybe, well I do drink a little. But, do I have a problem?

"You need help. Let me help you. We will save your life together."

AGE

HE SAVED MY LIFE:

I am just a teenager. I can't be an alcoholic. I just drink
a little. I am too young. Can you help me?

> Age: "Do you think about drinking all
> day long and look forward to later?"
> Who will get me some booze?
> Everyone drinks.

"Does it cause you any problems?"

> Well, not really. Maybe, I guess so.

"I will help you. I care!"
"I want the best for you. Don't try to fool me. I know.
I have been there. I have done it all!"

SPIRITUAL

HE SAVED MY LIFE:

I know the program. I have been here before. I know what I have to do. I just couldn't get the spiritual part of the program.

> Spiritual: Let's talk. What do you think?
> "God is the answer. He is my Higher Power. He is there for you! Surrender to Him. He will help you."

Many heart to heart conversations.

> Wow. What do I have to do?
> Surrender? Turn my will over to the power of God?

"Yes. It won't work any other way. You can't do it alone."

"Let go and let God!"

LAUGHTER

HE SAVED MY LIFE:

He taught me to laugh. A corny joke, a silly little game.
It is ok to smile.

> Laughter: A white haired man, a
> welcoming smile. A pat on the back. A
> warm feeling

He cares. He loves me. He jokes around.

> You mean I can have fun without alcohol?
> No way!

GIVING BACK

HE SAVED MY LIFE:

"What are you doing to give back to others?"

Well, I sponsor someone in the program.

"Yeah, what do you do for yourself?"

What should or could I do?

Giving back: "Come and share your story with others. Volunteer. Be there for others. Help others by helping yourself."

I couldn't do that, could I?
Yes, I guess I can.

Now I look forward to sharing with others. With a smile, I go to share my story one more time

SUPPORT

HE SAVED MY LIFE:

Yes, I am calling again today. I just needed to touch base with you again. I am doing ok today.

> Support: Hello again.
> "One day at a time. You can do it. Call anytime. We will be here for you."

"Hello. How is it really going today?"
> Not too bad. Thanks for being there.

"No problem. We can talk anytime."
> Good! Talk to you later.

CARING

HE SAVED MY LIFE:

He broke down when I told him Jim had passed. Is there any better tribute to a man's life that someone so lightly touched would be moved to tears at his loss?

> Caring: "Love lives on forever in each memory and thought of those who've shared our lives and all the happiness they've brought."—*American Greeting Card*

Love lives on forever. It never fades away. For in our hearts, our loved ones are with us every day."—*American Greeting Card*

He took a little light from the world when he left, and I am blessed from having known him.

COMPASSION

HE SAVED MY LIFE:

You are my friend. You treat me like an equal.
You show me compassion. You showed me love. You
showed me kindness.

> Compassion: Understanding the need
> for showing people that no matter where
> you are coming from or what you have
> done, you are a worthy person.

"You can be a friend. You can be loved. You deserve it.

God loves you and so do I."

SHARING

HE SAVED MY LIFE:

We shared conversation prior to a 5th step. We went to the room. We were introduced to the client. The young man was hugged and was wished well. That is the kind of thing he did. He was caring, supportive and kind. Peace!

> Sharing: A Fifth Step—The first time I did pretty well. I felt pretty good, but I didn't tell it all. Why wasn't this program working for me?

> "Is there anything still bothering you?"

Maybe. Ok, I'll do another Fifth Step.

-Relief. Freedom. Peace.

LOVE

HE SAVED MY LIFE:

What a beautiful difference one single life made. I loved him with all my heart. He will be missed.

Love: Why did I love him?

He truly cared for me.

He gave himself so I might grow.

He loved me for who I am—not who I was.

FAMILY

HE SAVED MY LIFE:

I will never forget how we were cared for as a family when we needed it. I am sure this is a sentiment that can be echoed a thousand times over. That is a remarkable legacy.

> Family: It is not just the alcoholic that suffers, but also the whole family becomes wrapped up in the disease. The family does not know how to help the alcoholic or help themselves.

It is a family disease.

A kind word—a pat on the shoulder.
"It will be alright. Let me give you a hug."

SOBRIETY

HE SAVED MY LIFE:

I didn't think I had a problem. I just used a little alcohol. "Be brave."

> Sobriety: Once I start drinking, I don't want to stop. I like how it feels. Then, no I don't. I can't get enough. I hate myself. All I can think about is my next drink.

> Must I admit I have a problem?

"Yes, I think you do have a problem. But, we can help you."

HUMOR

HE SAVED MY LIFE:

He took the time to talk to me about the way things are, not the way I thought they should be. He shot from the hip. I respected him for that.

> Humor: He had a sense of humor. His stories really hit home with me. That meant a lot to me.

He touched many lives. I thought very highly of him.The world and recovery community has lost a wonderful, insightful and caring man.

HELPLESSNESS

HE SAVED MY LIFE:

We brought our son. We were overwhelmed with such feelings of helplessness and not knowing how to help our young son with his drug and alcohol addictions.

> Helplessness: Jim was so caring and compassionate and gave us hope that day. He convinced us that our son could overcome his addictions.

It was so reassuring to meet someone who cared as much as we did. When our son left, Jim told us about his family. He was very proud of all of his family.
He had a great impact on our son's recovery. For that we will be forever grateful.

WORK

HE SAVED MY LIFE:

Working in the field of alcohol and chemical dependency was the joy of his life! He always had his patient's best interest in mind.

> Work: The chemical dependency field will certainly be lacking something without him.

But, Wow! Has Heaven become a better place because of him.

CHATS

HE SAVED MY LIFE:

I always enjoyed chatting with Jim. His kindness and love for people along with his sense of humor have touched many lives. He will be missed.

> Chats: Jim loved to talk. He enjoyed hearing the struggles and success stories of people around him. He had a way of knowing exactly how you were struggling and might help you overcome it.

He could talk to anyone just for fun or on a deep subject that might make a difference in one's life.

GOODBYE

HE SAVED MY LIFE:

Remembering Jim will last forever in my heart. He was the first man in AA who gently loved me unconditionally.

He saw my heart was broken and offered me his hand in recovery. He gave me the honor to share once a month in a meeting. He was my bridge to a happy and contented life because he gave it away to me and SAVED MY LIFE.

> Goodbye: Saying goodbye when it happens suddenly is painful and unbearable. Looking back on things can give hope for the future. He will be greatly missed but never will he leave my heart. His eyes told his whole story.

He shared his soul with me and for that I was so grateful. I got to know him. Rest in peace my friend.

MEMORIES

HE SAVED MY LIFE:

Memories of love and friendship are treasures to carry with you always.

> Memories: When the Lord calls our loved ones home, he leaves a gift of memories in exchange. Memories are the treasures that we hold in our hearts so that we can always remember the ones we love.

Thanks Jim for caring.

INSPIRATION

HE SAVED MY LIFE:

He made a big difference in my life. He showed me some inspiration for staying sober.

> Inspiration: Having someone who has been there and knows the "ropes" so to speak, is a big part of staying sober.

Being able to talk to someone or attend meetings can be a real inspiration to those who struggle daily. He was a great man and friend.

GRATITUDE

HE SAVED MY LIFE:

Simply put, Jim SAVED MY LIFE. I met him when he was working at an outpatient center. Over the next few weeks, Jim explained that I was an alcoholic, but with help, I could live a sober life. I have been sober ever since.

> Gratitude: I feel the deepest gratitude to Jim and how he has helped me the last several years. I am grateful for the person, the program and the people who work together to find sobriety and to keep their sobriety.

I am grateful to Jim and will miss him greatly.

ORDAINED

HE SAVED MY LIFE:

Jim made an impression on me.

> Ordained: He was certainly ordained to pass on the message of sobriety and freedom from bondage!

> He without a doubt has helped countless people.

I know Jim is happy and content in the presence of the Lord!

ENCOURAGEMENT

HE SAVED MY LIFE:

Every day he would tell me, "Have I told you I loved you yet, kid?" It always made my day!

> Encouragement: Through his positive influences and making others feel needed and wanted, he truly helped so SO many people including me!

It won't be the same without him.

SPECIAL

HE SAVED MY LIFE:

Jim was a very special person and will always be alive in many people's hearts and souls. He touched more people than anyone will ever know. He was one of God's angels and will not be forgotten. Jim has brought happiness and joy into our lives and will always have a special spot in our hearts. He has given us the gift of loving people without judgment and we will miss him always.

> Special: "A life well-lived is a precious gift of hope and strength and grace from someone who has made our world a brighter, better place."

"A life well-lived is a legacy of joy and pride and pleasure, a loving lasting memory our grateful hearts will treasure." *Hallmark Card.*

BLESSINGS

HE SAVED MY LIFE:

Jim was and still is a great help to me in our program.

> Blessings: God bless you for sharing
> your husband and your father with so
> many of us.

He was a true blessing to us all.

INCREDIBLE

HE SAVED MY LIFE:

Jim was an incredible, inspirational man who was taken from us far too soon.

> Incredible: Jim was a wonderful gift in many of our lives. He had an incredible understanding of the alcoholic and the needs of others.

He will be greatly missed.

HOPE

HE SAVED MY LIFE:

Belief in God and the good in all of us made the world a better place for having known Jim.

> Hope: I believe that hope survives, love prevails, tears cleanse, memories comfort, faith sooths, good thoughts reassure and that our belief in a better place calms the heart.

We loved Jim very much.

FRIENDSHIP

HE SAVED MY LIFE:

It is amazing that he was a friend of my first husband and years later was a friend of my second husband with no help from me!!! Goes to show how easy he was to be a friend.

> Friendship: Jim was a friend to many. He genuinely cared about how you were doing today. He would often ask, "How is that working for you?"

He made people feel special.

ANGEL

HE SAVED MY LIFE:

Jim was one of the "angels" at Tallgrass who SAVED MY LIFE!

> Angel: Jim seemed to have help from his higher power, who he chose to call God, when he talked to people. He always seemed to see the potential in people instead of the bad.

I will forever be grateful to Jim.

MENTOR

HE SAVED MY LIFE:

We had more in common than alcoholism.

> Mentor: We loved to talk sports. Jim was a man that gave me hope. He was a mentor, but most importantly, a friend.

HOME

HE SAVED MY LIFE:

Jim was a good friend to me for over 25 years. "He carried the message".

> Home: "When God calls his children home, their angels come to take them by the hand, leading them along a shining path into a place of peace and light. Home at last, they see the Lord open his arms welcoming them with a smile into the everlasting joy that is His love." *Ambassador Card*

DRUGGIES

HE SAVED MY LIFE:

Jim was a wonderful soul. He will be missed here on earth, but Heaven will be a better place.

> Druggies: I am sure he is talking to the druggies and drunks up there in Heaven.

ADMIRATION

HE SAVED MY LIFE:

Jim helped me early on in my recovery and inspired and helped me gain access to speak at the prison.

> Admiration: I have always had nothing
> but admiration and love for Jim. He was
> a great man.

GENTLENESS

HE SAVED MY LIFE:

What a neat man Jim was! I got to visit with him several times during his last week.

> Gentleness: He had a kind and gentle heart. He was always kind to the alcoholic and others with addictions. He loved those in need.

He will be greatly missed by the whole recovery community.

IMPRINTS

HE SAVED MY LIFE:

Jim touched this world in a big way. He served others through his work, his kindness and his humor.

> Imprints: "A great soul serves everyone
> all the time. "A great soul never dies. It
> brings us together again and again."

"Each life touches this world in a way no others can—leaving not only wonderful memories, but lasting imprints in our hearts." *Maya Angelou*

RESPECT

HE SAVED MY LIFE:

Jim was a caring person who listened to my venting when things were not going well in my workday. I missed him greatly when he moved on to a new job.

> Respect: Being a co-worker at the penitentiary, we frequently sat together at the chow hall and shared our thoughts and complaints over the food we were eating. Jim was respected so much for his caring and compassionate dealings with clients.

He is always with you. Love lives on forever in the heart.

MEETINGS

HE SAVED MY LIFE:

We were truly blessed to know and love Jim in the fellowship of A.A.

> Meetings: Attending meetings was the cornerstone of his sobriety. He knew he depended on the program and people there to keep him on the right track toward a sober life.

Friendships and conversation were needed for him to stay sober.

He loved the fellowship.

RECOVERY

HE SAVED MY LIFE:

Jim was a wonderful part of my recovery. I am grateful to have gotten to know and to love him. I will miss him dearly.

> Recovery: Many components make recovery successful. Jim was a person who thrived on helping those who also suffered from the disease. He was grateful for each person who tried to find sobriety. He became very knowledgeable about "seeing" where a person was coming from in his or her life in the world of alcohol or other addictions.

"Some souls pass through this life line
Like a gentle summer rain.
They touch our hearts and then return
To Heaven once again." *Hallmark Expressions*

DEDICATED

HE SAVED MY LIFE:

Jim was a wonderful man and very dedicated to his cause. He was there for us on several occasions. He will be greatly missed.

> Dedicated: Jim was a great counselor and a good man.

"The world will never be the same because of the beautiful difference one life has made." *American Greetings*

"The loss is immeasurable, but, also immeasurable in the love left behind." *Felecia Moran*

"Sometimes the words are hard to find—But warm thoughts are always there." *Expressions-Hallmark*

BOND

HE SAVE MY LIFE:

I had a special bond with Jim. We could sit and talk and understand each other's struggles. I always felt close to him.

Bond: One on one was one of Jim's favorite ways to communicate. The conversation was personal and could become more than a superficial non-personal discussion. He liked to dig deep and get to the real stuff.

CHEERLEADER

HE SAVED MY LIFE:

I loved Jim's smile and lean in from the side, looking at you, hug.

Cheerleader: He always cheered me up. He always knew how I felt before I spoke.

He was a great loving man and will be greatly missed.

RECOVERY

HE SAVED MY LIFE:

He was the wise kind soul in the rooms of recovery for me.

> Recovery: Many times Jim told his story
> or listened to others as they worked to
> find recovery for themselves.

After finding recovery for myself, I worked with him and he became a trusted friend who spoke the truth and loved to laugh.

TRUTH

HE SAVED MY LIFE:

I could always count on him to speak truth and love to me.

> Truth: Jim always said it like it was when asked about alcoholism in his life. If you asked him a question, he would answer exactly what he thought. He did this with love and caring.

I look forward to seeing him again.

CONTINUOUS SOBRIETY

HE SAVED MY LIFE:

Jim's dedication to his sobriety by always being there for others is partly responsible for my 26 years of continuous sobriety.

> Continuous Sobriety: It is not easy to stay sober, but working the program, following the steps, sponsoring someone and doing your part in service will help accomplish your goals.

God speed, Jim.

BELIEF

HE SAVED MY LIFE:

He SAVED MY LIFE when I didn't want it saved. He believed in me when I had no intentions of believing in myself.

> Belief: Not being able to accept who you are and the things done in your past makes it very hard to believe in yourself. He helped me feel worthy of accepting who I am.

I loved him so very much.

CARING

HE SAVED MY LIFE:

Jim always said he loved me no matter how often I saw him.

> Caring: Jim had a way of letting others know he loved them in spite of themselves. He truly cared for the alcoholic and drug addict.

He understood the struggles and trials they were going through.

FATHER FIGURE

HE SAVED MY LIFE:

I worked with Jim. He taught me a lot about adolescents and about birds.

> Father figure: Jim often said he felt he was like a father figure to many of the adolescents he worked with as a counselor. He knew they needed a person who was loving and caring.

When we had free time, we talked about birds. He always talked about sitting outside at his house watching the birds.

I like birds too, so we had good talks.

WELCOMING

HE SAVED MY LIFE:

So many memories, where do I begin? I was one of the first to enter Tallgrass. He was the first person that greeted me when I walked through the door. His BLUE eyes and welcome was the warmest welcome.

> Welcoming: He loved greeting people and putting them at ease with his easy going manner. He ended up being not just a friend, but a mentor and co-worker.

I am so grateful to say he was at our wedding. We have had many conversations. All were with God involved.

He loved his kids.
He talked so proudly of them.

Thanks, Jim.
Your friend always.

COUNSELOR

HE SAVED MY LIFE:

Jim was my first counselor 27 years ago. He helped me through my alcoholism and helped me love again.

> Counselor: He was a great counselor.
> He gave of himself.

There is one hell of a meeting going on in Heaven!

CONVERSATIONALIST

HE SAVED MY LIFE:

We were not related by blood, but he was my brother through the program. I remember the first time I saw him after I entered the program. He gave me a big hug and welcomed me with open arms.

> Conversationalist: We had great talks.
> We could talk for hours. Nobody knows
> the cost until you have walked the walk.
> Thanks, Jim.

ENCOURAGEMENT

HE SAVED MY LIFE:

Thanks for your quiet, warmth and sincere (with a pat on the shoulder) encouragement of it will be OK.
I will never forget our last encounter.

> Encouragement: The pat on the shoulder, the look in the eye, the firm hugs were all ways for him to encourage others no matter how the day was going for them or him. Many people looked forward to a hug.

Everyone needs a hug sometimes you know. Man, woman and child, they all looked forward to this simple feeling of being accepted in an imperfect world.

TIME

HE SAVED MY LIFE:

Thanks for sharing your husband, father and grandfather with me. You let him spend time with people who needed someone—like me or someone who needed to be hugged at the right time.

> Time: Jim always had time to help anyone in need of assistance in the recovery circle. Nothing would please him more than going to help someone who may need him.

Jim was a very important part of my recovery life. Jim was one of the people who had THOSE eyes to his soul who made me want to recover.

Jim will be greatly missed, but I want you to know he will always be a very special person in my life and always in my recovery.

FEELINGS

GRANDPA JIM—(JAMES)

You made everyone feel SPECIAL.

> Feelings: One example is a cat named
> Duchess. You made her feel like a queen.

I loved farming with you.

You also made great bread—Sometimes even perfect bread.

I will always love you and remember the memories we had together.

I love (heart) U Grandpa. From Megan

THE 13ᵀᴴ STEP—FORGIVING HIMSELF

HE LOVED US:

It was difficult for him to show us he cared. We don't know why really. He tried to love us. He just couldn't cross over to the "13ᵗʰ" step—forgiving himself.

> Pain: Sometimes he was angry—
> Sometimes he was in pain.

The world without alcohol was not always easy. He did not desire to drink—That was taken from him. Thank you God for giving him sobriety.

> Knowledge: He knew all the right answers.—He knew the big book from cover to cover. He believed in the power of God.

He could and did help hundreds of people.—But, he struggled in an imperfect world.

Forgiving himself: Accepting the gifts God had given him. Insight, cunning sense of knowing.

> Struggles: Forgiving himself, Truthfulness, Other addictions.

Feeling worthy of things in the world. Taking responsibility.

He hated telling lies.

> Health: He hated having diabetes. He hated taking pills.

He hated not feeling his hands and feet.
He hated the idea of being a burden to someone.

> Love and Forgiveness: We loved him, but did not always understand him.

God heard his pleas and took him home.

He is free. He is whole. He is in the loving arms of Jesus!

THE 13TH STEP—FORGIVEN

_____

_____

_____

_____

_____

_____

_____

_____

SPECIAL MEMORIES OF JIM STONEALL

_____

_____

_____

_____

_____

_____

_____

_____

A TRUSTED FRIEND

Well, here we go. Jim and I met when he was a Drug and Alcohol Counselor at the South Dakota State Penitentiary some 15 years ago. Jim was my guy that got me through security which was complicated due to a prior felony drug conviction of mine. Jim worked tirelessly to get me clearance and finally got it. Then every time he would get a new officer in charge he would go through the same thing. He kept a large file on me with tape-recorded testimonies from former probation officers etc . . . in it and would resubmit it over and over again.

After Jim left the penitentiary, I would see him at different recovery related events around Sioux Falls. He was always a staunch ambassador for the recovery process. He was very selfless in his commitment in helping the newcomer. No matter where I would see

Jim, he would have a smile on his face and his job was related to helping someone finding sobriety in his or her life. It was his mission.

I was proud to have Jim Stoneall as a mentor in my life and even prouder to call him my friend. He is greatly missed in the recovery circles in Sioux Falls and forever loved for his love of the addict still suffering.

Sincerely—Greg Sands—Clean Date: 3-17-19

FRIEND AND COLLEAGUE

I always say that I am never grateful enough for the people that were in the program when I came into the fellowship. Jim was one of those people. He would always listen to whatever was troubling me or what was on my mind. As years went by, I would refer people seeking help to him and he would refer them to me if they were in need of a sponsor or a friend. We live in a busy world and sometimes a period of time would go by and we would not see each other, but when we did see each other it was like a breath of fresh air. When we parted Jim would always say, "I miss you my friend and I love you." Not many men say that to each other.

He was a wonderful man that had recovery and "carrying the message" on his heart. He was what this program is all about. I miss him as I do many others that have left and are in a better place. I Love you Jim.

Ron T.

TRUSTED FRIEND

Jim became more than a trusted friend from our church when our son developed a methamphetamine habit, buying, selling, and using. As our son became more involved, we depended on Jim for advice and answers to our questions. Jim was almost always there at church with a hug and a smile for us. We missed him when he wasn't there.

The best advice he ever gave us was to "keep on praying and never give up on your son." Jim became someone who understood the fears we had about prison life and what was happening to our son and our family. He was someone who cared about our son and us.

I believe that Jim prayed for us and I know he loved us through all six years of prison visits. Jim was here to rejoice with us when our son was released from prison, came home, and put his life back together again.

Jim was a trusted friend we could and did confide in and he always encouraged us. He was a wonderful counselor. We are sorry that Jim had to leave this earth so early and so suddenly, but we know he is in heaven and "hugging us" from there. Thank you, Jim. We miss you.

Sue Larson

MY TIME WITH JIM

I heard we were hiring a guy from Keystone Treatment Center and his name was Jim Stoneall. The name was familiar. I had met Jim sometime before through some AA function. During our journey together, one day in May, I met him for the first time at Tallgrass. I believe his daughter-in-law was with him. We greeted each other. He was very happy to be coming to work at Tallgrass. He showed her around the property and when he got ready to leave said goodbye and that he would see me when he started work.

There are so many memories I have about Jim. I am going to share a few that really stick out. Some are humorous and some are serious. I will start with the humorous.

The first task that I remember giving Jim was to assemble a couple of trellises that we had purchased. If my memory serves me right, I remember Jim telling me that he would not have any trouble assembling them. He assured me that he was mechanically inclined and wouldn't have any trouble with the task. I wouldn't say that he didn't have any mechanical ability, but I would say that his idea and my idea of his ability were a little different. What took him a day and a half to do would have taken me about a half of a day. Later, when Jim would offer me a hand doing something involving tools, I would remind him that I needed to have it done in a timely manner, but thanks anyway. He would respond with some kind words or some sort of gesture.

One day I came to work and a fellow employee came to me with a big smile on his face and said he needed to share something with me. It seems that Jim had stopped by work for a short time. He went to leave and came back and said that someone had taken his car. It was gone. They asked Jim where he parked the car and he said it was in front of the house in a parking spot. They went out and looked for his car and found it in the bottom up against a tree. He insisted that he put his car in park and pulled the keys. For a while, we would do a checklist when he came to work to see where he parked his car, had his keys and that the car was where he said he parked it. Once again Jim responded with some kind words or the proper gesture.

One of the coolest things I remember was his ability to listen to people. He would share things with them that would help them work through a problem they were having in their life at that time. He seemed to have some uncanny ability to have a read on something without knowing all the facts. He was always willing to give time to people when they wanted to talk to him.

My personal relationship with Jim was amazing. He always thanked me for being in his life, but I can tell you that he did so much more for me than he ever realized. He taught me things about working with people in a relatively short period of time that would have taken years to learn on my own. To quote Jim, "How is that working for you?" became the most common saying at Tallgrass. Everyone understood where the saying came from. Jim showed me what it really meant to love your family. He was so proud of his kids. He would always talk about the activities they were involved in school and how proud he was of them. He would share about their accomplishments. He was grateful for them allowing him to be part of their lives. When it came to Veronica, I don't believe I ever heard Jim say a cruel or mean thing about her. He was very proud of her accomplishments and talked about them often. They included her teaching, singing, being an artist and her writing gifts. They were important in his life. There wasn't a day that went by that he wasn't sharing something about his wife, kids or grandkids. One of the biggest highlights that I remember him being excited about was their trip to San Diego and going to "The Price is Right" and wearing the shirts that Veronica made.

I remember the day that Jim died. It was a Tuesday. We had a tough winter and Jim would go home after work and move snow. He left work around 4pm and said he was going to go home and get on the tractor to move some snow and would see us tomorrow if the roads were open and he could get to work. By the way, his tractor was his pride and joy and consumed a lot of conversation at work. I was at a meeting later that night and received a call from Mike saying that Jim's son, Jameson Stoneall had called to say his dad had a massive heart attack and had died. I was at a loss for words. All I could do was go back to my meeting and tell everyone what had happened. I headed back to work because I knew I needed to be there. Once people found out Jim was gone, there would be a lot of phone calls. It was a very tough few days at work. I can tell you that Jim had such an effect on people that there was an outpouring of people reaching out to Tallgrass. They wanted to help in any way they could. It was amazing.

Jim attended a 5:30 pm AA meeting on Wednesdays. Each week he sat in the same chair. On the day after Jim died, we were at this regular 5:30 meeting. No one sat in the chair where he would normally sit. The meeting was a very healing process as we all discussed how Jim had touched our lives. It was amazing how Jim touched every person he encountered.

My perspective is from the recovery side, but I do know that Jim had an impact on people who were not in recovery also. I cannot say enough about Jim and how his life truly touched numbers and numbers of people. I will be forever grateful for having the privilege to know Jim and be included in his life. Jim has touched my life and has shown me what it means to give of myself so others may have a better life. Until I get to see Jim in the big meeting, I will try to live the example that Jim has shown me.

Bob Livingston, Friend and co-worker

NEIGHBOR AND FRIEND

A tribute to Jim—given at the prayer service

Meeting Jim was proof of the adage, "what you see is what you get". While he was many things to the different people in his life, the word that best describes who he was to me was REAL. I don't think Jim spent a lot of time worrying about what people thought about him. Rather, he tried to be true to his beliefs and values—and let the chips fall where they may. But, if you cared to inquire about his viewpoint on a subject, he was always VERY clear on his thoughts.

One of the first times I met him where we were spending time visiting was at his home when he and Veronica and Dale and I were together. I remember he spoke openly about the fact that he was a recovering alcoholic. He didn't sugar coat it—in fact, I recall he said he'd been a drunk for to many years. I was a bit taken back by his frankness and possibly a bit uncomfortable. After all, it is not socially acceptable to speak openly about one's inner struggles—past or present—is it? If you were fortunate enough to have known Jim, you would know that he was much less concerned about being socially acceptable, and a whole lot more focused on his life's ambition. That was to make society and individuals aware that there could be productive life following treatment for addictions. He dedicated his life toward understanding, treating and rehabilitating those struggling with the pain of addiction. Most surely they have lost a champion.

In addition to his deep faith in Jesus Christ, he was devoted to his family. He was immensely proud of Jameson, Scott, and Heather and deeply loved his grandchildren. He glowed when he spoke of Veronica as well. He was looking forward to meeting a new grandchild through adoption.

Jim knew about fighting personal demons in his life and he had both understanding and empathy for those dealing with similar issues. Sometimes I really wondered if Jim didn't have a built in radar system alerting him to those who were having a tough time. During our Kyle's yearlong battle with cancer, he would make a beeline to me after the morning church service. "How are you doin'? he'd ask looking me squarely in the face. "Fine," I'd usually mumble upon which I'd get that intense look and he'd respond, "That's great—How are you REALLY doing?"

That was Jim. He and Veronica had walked that walk, having lost a dear nephew after a long hard fought battle with cancer.

Then—there were the hugs. I was raised in an era where any form of personal contact was highly suspect. Maybe, at funerals or weddings and I got used to the church ladies giving hugs, but one day along comes this intense looking guy with white hair, and he gives me a serious hug? No questions asked! I thought to myself, "What was that????"

Jim Stoneall is what that was! And again, he seemed to have that radar thing going, and knew who needed a hug. I got one last Sunday. We will miss those hugs!!

Tuesday night after receiving the news of his passing, I went to bed and tried to make sense of losing someone so special, so young, with so much yet undone. I just could not. I prayed, "Lord, I just don't understand." Then it came to me that I was focusing on the loss and hurt of those of us left behind. I needed to focus on the fact that Jim is home where he belongs. Our Kyle knew and respected Jim, and as I drifted off to sleep, I had this picture in my mind. Kyle was welcoming Jim home. I could almost hear him say, "Hey, Jim! Welcome to the celebration."

In the midst of our grief and feelings of loss, we are reminded of the promise we have of eternal life in Heaven through Jesus. And, with that hope, comes peace. Thanks be to God!

By Kathy Thorpe

TRIBUTE AT THE FUNERAL SERVICE

Good morning. I am going to read most of this so I don't lose my train of thought, which Jim and I could do with great frequency, as you know.

On Tuesday out of nowhere expected, the word of Jim's death spread quietly through the community of recovery. The next day shocked and with a real sense of loss, we gathered at our regularly scheduled 5:30 Wednesday afternoon recovery meeting. In a packed room of the recovering individuals, there was an empty chair where Jim had been sitting for many years. We individually shared, and cried and let it go. Let it out. Jim was a valued member, a member for almost 30 years, and a genuine and valued human being. We loved Jim. Jim loved you.

When I first met Jim, around 1982, he was not the man that he had become over the years.

I never knew the man on the cover of the service bulletin, the dark haired man, and the guy with a smile. When I first met him, the man I met in those early days was gray, mad and very resentful of where this disease had taken him. And he wasn't afraid to tell you how mad he really was or what he thought of you. There was a sincere sadness about him as is often the case with most individuals that are taken with this disease called alcoholism.

Through the later years and with continued sobriety, however, Jim's sense of humor and mischief resurfaced, as you well know. He laughed and was able to connect with people as he shared his experience, strength and hope. As Jim continued his work and developed his skills as a counselor, he developed a million dollar nose for smelling alcoholic BS. He could smell it just walking up to them. He was not afraid to get in your face and or to bring it on to break down the delusion that was associated with the disease of alcoholism.

Jim was not a gossip. I considered him a "secret keeper". There are a lot of people from the recovery world in this room and they know that he was a man who was trusted to share their dirty laundry or private feelings on the table. He could maintain confidentiality. He had thousands of conversations over his career. He had earned his chair in recovery from his own failures and success in the program. He was a handsome devil.

He was a diabetic. Often, we would go to dinner following our 5:30 meeting. He would bail into a large order of fettuccini Alfredo with shrimp. He would grin right through the dinner experience often with a blob of cheese sauce on his shirt or mouth. He was known for this as the family reflected last night. We knew that, too. He never did buy that spot remover did he? He loved his deserts. He carefully tried to monitor his blood sugar, but he could not walk by a good desert.

He loved his wife's abilities as a teacher and an artist. He loved his children and his grandchildren. He loved his church community. He loved the church couples group. Some of you may have been a part of that group. He truly loved that weekly meeting.

He loved to tell stories, often with excruciating minute details. Long winded, Jim what was your point?

Did I say?

He loved his wife, his children and his grandchildren. We got it, Jim. We got it. He could not shut up about you guys.

Now this is interesting. I think he liked haircuts. At least his sister-in-law did. I tried in later years to get him to grow a ponytail and the hair out. I think he actually considered it. I really do. He smiled when I suggested it.

Others had mentioned his great affection for a clean and orderly car. Sparkling interior, he truly needed to invent an organizer for the thousands of items on the floor, on the seat and stuck to the inside of the windshield. The interior of this car was paralleled to the archeological site on the discovery channel.

What a beauty. Boy, he was a beauty. I would suggest a car wash. He would say, "I live on a gravel road." Then he would smile. The badge of honor as the family knows. They say he looked for the oldest cars so he could fix those cars. They shared that last night.

One final comment.

Jim had a collective wisdom one learned and EARNED by a daily commitment in a daily struggle. He did not take his sobriety for granted.

Anybody that knows Jim knows he was challenged on a daily basis to grow in God's grace and rededicate his life to the spiritual program of 12-step recovery.

Now, I know Jim would want me to suggest to individuals that are suffering from problems relating to Alcoholism and drug addiction, he would want me to tell you that there is a solution. All right? So, I am going to do that. I did that. He would not want me to miss this opportunity to tell you about it.

There are statistically one out of ten in this room that are suffering from the problems related to alcohol and addictions. There is a solution and Jim found it.

Now, I ask you in closing to close your eyes and listen to a selection from the text, from the text of Alcoholics Anonymous.

This was Jim's struggle and this was his success.

I am going to paraphrase this by changing one word only.

Please close your eyes and imagine Jim saying this to you. (From the Blue Book)

"The last 30 years of my life have been rich and meaningful. I have had my share of problems, heartaches and disappointments, because that is life, but also I have known a great deal of joy, and a peace that is the handmaiden of an inner freedom. I have a wealth of friends and, with my AA friends, an unusual quality of fellowship. For, to these people, I am truly related. First, through mutual pain and despair and later through mutual objectives and new found faith and hope. And, as the years go by, working together, sharing our experiences with one another, and also sharing a mutual trust, understanding and love—without strings, without obligation—we acquire relationships that are unique and priceless."

"There is no more "aloneness," with that awful ache, so deep in the heart of every alcoholic that nothing before, could ever reach it. That ache is gone and never need return again.

Now there is a sense of belonging, of being wanted and needed and loved. In return for a bottle and a hangover, I have been given the Keys of the Kingdom." Taken from the chapter "Keys to the Kingdom" in the Alcoholics Anonymous Book

by Tom Ashworth, a friend and colleague

_____

_____

_____

_____

_____

_____

_____

_____

PRAYER SERVICE TRIBUTES

_____

_____

_____

_____

_____

_____

_____

_____

FRIEND AND MENTOR

Jim came into my life about four years ago. Jim was a mentor to me. I loved Jim and Jim loved me. He had a little memory problem. He parked his car outside and couldn't find it when he went to leave. Jim said his car "jumped out of park" and went down the hill. It missed the trellis and the pine tree. He was my dear buddy.

Bob Livingston—Friend and co-worker

COUNSELOR AND FRIEND

Jim came into my life 27 years ago. He was my first counselor.

He helped me through alcoholism and helped me love again.

He gave of himself. There is one hell of a meeting going on in Heaven.

Dan Everett—friend

FATHER-IN-LAW

Jim was my father for 20 years. Hugs you know. He was the guy who made perfect bread for Sunday dinner. He loved sports and loved his grandkids. He was so proud of each of his children. He will always be missed.

Through my work, I had opportunity to see and meet many people in AA. I am happy that many of them are here to support and honor Jim as well as many other people.

Tracey Stoneall—daughter-in-law

BROTHER-IN-LAW

Jim and I had some fun times too. We played on the same softball team. I was a gopher pitcher and threw a pitch. The batter hit it hard. Jim ran and ran to catch the ball, but in the process ran into the fence. He cut his nose and had a scar to prove it. Jim was a competitor. He was great.

Kent Scott-brother-in-law

SISTER-IN-LAW

Jim and Veronica started dating and had a whorl-wind romance.

They would come to my apartment. In early marriage, Jim would call me to borrow some K2R spot remover. Jim always had a spot on his tie. They never bought any! My mom called me Betsy Poo, Veronica called me Sister Poo and Jim shortened it to just Poo.

We always talked one on one as we cut his hair. We had a strong bond. We thank the Lord for taking him on his feet. My son, Erik greeted him in Heaven.

Dorene Gaard-sister-in-law

NEIGHBOR AND FRIEND

We would go back and forth helping each other. We lived just a couple miles apart. I was going to build a garage and Jim came with his old tractor to help. It didn't have very good breaks. I am not sure how but we did get the garage built. It was a challenge, but we got it up and it is still standing today.

Dale Thorpe-Neighbor and friend

SON #2

My first best memories were about sports. We were in a lot of different sports and he was always there. Even for the track meets. I wasn't very good. I ran the mile and always came in last or 2nd to last. He always talked to everyone. I admired his ability to talk, like at our wedding reception. He was able to talk without really thinking about it.

Scott Stoneall—son

SISTER

I thought you might like to hear a little about his younger days. I was the first one to drive the Allis Charmers tractor. I was the oldest. I remember Jim as an avid gardener. He was not so good at weeding as a child, but loved to plant.

He was a good athlete. He played football and could tell you the play by play many years later. He also ran in track. He got off the school bus and ran home so he could have track training. His dad would want him home to do chores so this was a way he could participate.

Kathy Hibbert—sister

SON #1

I'm the other son. We would have conversation about things and people from George, Iowa. I would have no idea what he was talking about. For some reason, we clashed. Both of us were stubborn. One time I remember traveling for eight or nine hours in the car together. We were going to watch Scott wrestle. We were one on one—in the car. He did most of the talking. It was one of my best memories.

Jameson Stoneall—son

DAUGHTER

Thanks for being here. It is awesome to hear the stories.

I clashed with Dad. We were both strong willed.

One memory I have is we had gone into town. I asked him if we could have ice cream. He said yes, but it will be the last one you get this year! I thought, "Oh, no!" Then he said it was New Year's Eve!

I worked with my Dad fixing cars. He always picked the oldest cars in the world. I learned a lot about cars that way. In college, I studied Architecture and needed to build a wall for one of my classes. I came home and together we got it done. Thank you all for being here tonight.

Heather Stoneall—Daughter

NIECE

Jim was excited when I entered the program. We had many great talks.

For people from Tallgrass, Jim was so excited to go to work for Tallgrass. He looked forward to no paper work and just talking to people. He was filled with joy!

Kami Scott-niece

DAUGHTER-IN-LAW

When I was dating Scott, I asked what his dad was like. He said he was a fellow extravert. Jim and I were both talkative. I was surprised when he talked more than I did! He really wanted to get to know people. He had piercing blue eyes, tight hugs.

One day I got a call from Jim. He wanted to check and find out if Scott was treating me with respect. He said to treat each other with respect and dignity and things will go well for you.

It is a bummer that he won't get to meet our new baby.

Suzy Stoneall—daughter-in-law

GRANDDAUGHTER

I am Jim's oldest granddaughter. When I was five or six years old, I came into the kitchen and saw him without his teeth. (big laugh) He told me how he lost his teeth and everything.

He loved me and I loved him. Go Grandpa!

Megan Stoneall—granddaughter

WIFE

Written late in the evening after Jim's death.

February 16, 2010. Jim died suddenly today. Thank you, Lord for surrounding me with family and friends. Through their prayers and support I feel the love and peace you offer through them.

Today was a sunny cold day. Jim was blessed with a day of work at TLC. He enjoyed working days. He loved his work. He chose to get up early. He was always excited about going to work. He would be able to use his gifts to help someone. This was his passion, his greatest gift and love. God had given him the gift of insight and love through the trials and joys of the disease of alcoholism. He worked all day. He smiled, laughed, joked and gave his love to those around him. This was his safe place, his element, his joy and his peace.

Jim came home early from work. He had started at 7:00 am not because he had to, but because he wanted to. He came home in a good mood. He smiled at me and said, "I'm going out and start the tractor and clear the snow. See you in a bit."

Jim often spent half an hour to an hour clearing snow and keeping his old tractor running. You had to crank it to start it. He loved the old tractor. It was his dad's.

I decided I should go out and see if he needed help. I walked out to the tractor and found him collapsed over the tractor. Oh, My God! No! I turned and ran back to the house, called 911 and went back outside.

Darkness fell, lights blinked, phone calls were made. God had taken him home.

No more tears. No more pain. He is free and enjoying a new life with Jesus.

Thanks be to God!

Veronica Stoneall